Romancing Me:
A GUIDE FOR MY GIRL

Marianne Pelletier, CTR

Wally the Wellwisher Press

Romancing Me: A Guide for My Girl
Marianne Pelletier, CTR

Copyright 2012 Marianne M. Pelletier
Wally the Wellwisher Press

ISBN-13: 978-0615581248
ISBN-10: 0615581242

Design and Artwork by Lighthouse24
Front Cover Photos by Yuri Arcurs/Bigstock
Back Cover Photo by Rashevskyi Viacheslav

Contents

Introduction	1
How to Use this Guide	3
About Me	**5**
In a Nutshell	7
Values	8
Desire	9
Image	9
Tastes	10
Routines	14
Us When We Communicate	**19**
Us In Public	**25**
What You Do That I Adore	**31**
Us At Home	**35**
Us When We Eat	**39**
Us Apart	**45**
Us and Gifts	**49**
Us and Sex	**57**
Wrap-Up	**63**
About the Author	67

Introduction

In my tarot practice, many men ask me if it's time for them to act on their feelings for a woman, and many women ask me when their man of interest will act. People call me to ask how another feels about them, even if one partner is cheating on the other.

I wrote this workbook, *A Guide for My Girl,* to help you talk to the woman in your life about your needs. The companion workbook, *Romancing Me: A Guide for My Man,* is to help your woman express herself to you.

How to Use this Guide

You don't have to answer all of the questions, or look at all the sections. Use the Guide to communicate with a loved one or dating partner. If any part doesn't make sense to you, then skip it (if you have suggestions, though, let me know at Marianne@tarotbymarianne.com). Add your own notes anywhere you feel like, especially if one of your choices would be a surprise to your girl.

Please use this book to open conversation, explore each other's needs, and say things that you have had trouble saying aloud. You may find that you'd like to try a little bit of leather in the bedroom, or breakfast in bed, or a risqué smooch in public. Wouldn't it be wonderful if your love interest is delighted by the idea?

About Me

– *In a Nutshell* –

I am:
- ❏ Visual – I love to look at things
- ❏ Auditory – I'm into the sound of things
- ❏ Tactile – I like what I can touch

My favorite color is: _____

My favorite sound is: _____

_____

My favorite fabric or sensation is: _____

_____

I am:
- ❏ Spontaneous
- ❏ Planful
- ❏ Laid back
- ❏ Control freaky
- ❏ Playful
- ❏ Quite/peaceful
- ❏ Committed/focused
- ❏ Quick
- ❏ A born again Christian
- ❏ I describe myself this way: _____

_____

– *Values* –

What I value most is:

- ❏ Wealth
- ❏ Love
- ❏ Fame
- ❏ Beauty
- ❏ Intelligence
- ❏ Accomplishment
- ❏ Courage
- ❏ Respect
- ❏ Family
- ❏ My career
- ❏ Fun
- ❏ Extravagance
- ❏ Frugality
- ❏ Intellect
- ❏ Justice
- ❏ Joy/happiness
- ❏ Open mindedness
- ❏ Tradition
- ❏ Opulence
- ❏ Fresh airy
- ❏ Excitement
- ❏ Sex
- ❏ My religious or spiritual practice
- ❏ Something else: _____

_____

– *Desires* –

What I want most from a relationship is:
- ❏ Validation
- ❏ Respect
- ❏ Love
- ❏ Family
    - ❏ Including children
- ❏ Fun
- ❏ Companionship
- ❏ Pride
- ❏ Sex

❏ Something else: _____

_____

– *Image* –

I want to be seen as:
- ❏ Fair
- ❏ Powerful
- ❏ Wise
- ❏ Strong
- ❏ Excitement
- ❏ Rich
- ❏ Brave
- ❏ Funny
- ❏ Loving
- ❏ Dependable
- ❏ This: _____

_____

- Image - (continued)

When I dress, it's for:
- ❑ Comfort
- ❑ Style
- ❑ Function
- ❑ Expression of my power/wealth
- ❑ Expression of my creativity
- ❑ This: _____

_____

– Tastes –

I have a:
- ❑ Sweet tooth
- ❑ Salt tooth
- ❑ Focus on healthy eating
- ❑ Taste that runs this way: _____

_____

Around alcohol, I am:
- ❑ Not a drinker
- ❑ A beer man
- ❑ A wine man
- ❑ A liquor man
- ❑ A mixed drink man, especially: _____

_____

- ❑ A man who drinks mostly: _____

_____

- Tastes - (continued)

For entertainment, I:
- ❏ Enjoy the theater
- ❏ Would be really making a sacrifice to go to a play or musical
- ❏ Like museums
- ❏ Would rather not go to museums
- ❏ Like opera
- ❏ Like concerts

Please don't ever make me go to: _____

_____

I would really be delighted to get tickets for: ___

_____

When it comes to sports, I:
- ❏ Play sports
- ❏ Watch sports
- ❏ Play sports on my gadget: _____

_____

- ❏ Have a fantasy sports team: _____

_____

- ❏ Can take or leave sports
- ❏ Hate sports
- ❏ My favorite sport to play: _____

_____

- ❏ My favorite sport to watch: _____

_____

(list continues . . .)

- Tastes - (continued)

❏ My favorite team: _____

_____

I also:

❏ Dig music:
   My favorite styles:
   ❏ Rock
   ❏ Rap
   ❏ Symphonic
   ❏ Jazz
   ❏ Country
   ❏ Christian
   ❏ Hip-hop
   ❏ Softer stuff
   ❏ Folk
   ❏ Blue grass
   ❏ This: _____

   _____

   ❏ I play an instrument: _____

   _____

   ❏ I play an air: _____

   _____

❏ Like movies:
   ❏ At home
   ❏ At the theatre
   ❏ On my gadget: _____

   _____

   (list continues . . .)

- Tastes - (continued)

❏ My favorite movie genre is:___
_____

❏ My favorite movie is: _____
_____

❏ Like the outdoors
  ❏ My favorite outdoor activity is:
_____

Politically, I lean:
  ❏ Left
  ❏ Middle
  ❏ Right
  ❏ Not into this kind of label

  And I am:
    ❏ Not interested in politics
    ❏ Registered as | ❏ Akin to
      ❏ Democrats
      ❏ Republicans
      ❏ Independents
      ❏ This party: _____

For religion, I practice:
  ❏ Christianity
  ❏ Judaism
  ❏ Buddhism
  ❏ Wiccan
  ❏ This: _____
  (list continues . . .)

- Tastes - (continued)

❏ I'm spiritual more than religious
❏ I don't believe in that stuff

My astrological sign is:
❏ Not important to me
❏ Aries
❏ Taurus
❏ Gemini
❏ Cancer
❏ Leo
❏ Virgo
❏ Libra
❏ Scorpio
❏ Sagittarius
❏ Capricorn
❏ Aquarius
❏ Pisces

– Routines –

I have the most energy in the:
❏ Morning
❏ Afternoon
❏ Evening
❏ Nighttime

These are my hobbies:
❏ Electronics: _____

❏ Games: _____

(list continues . . .)

- *Routines - (continued)*

- ❏ Trains/mini-vehicles: _____

  _____

- ❏ Models/Legos/building something: __

  _____

- ❏ Cards/Magic/Dungeons: _____

  _____

- ❏ Online gaming:
    - ❏ Gambling
    - ❏ Fantasy
    - ❏ This: _____

- ❏ Reading, especially: _____

  _____

- ❏ Dancing: _____
- ❏ Woodworking or building/making: __

  _____

- Gardening:
    - ❏ Flowers
    - ❏ Food
    - ❏ This: _____
- ❏ Cars:
    - ❏ Driving
    - ❏ Fixing
    - ❏ Looking at
    - ❏ My favorite car: _____

  _____

(list continues . . .)

- Routines - (continued)

- ❏ Shooting:
    - ❏ Pool
    - ❏ Skeet
    - ❏ Target
    - ❏ Archery
    - ❏ Hunting
    - ❏ Tin cans in my back yard
    - ❏ Doesn't matter as long as it's fun
- ❏ Photography:
    - ❏ Digital
    - ❏ Film
    - ❏ I like to photograph: _____

    _____
- ❏ Collecting: _____
- ❏ Camping, especially at: _____

    _____
- ❏ Backpacking:
    - ❏ Into the woods
    - ❏ Up mountains
    - ❏ Rock climbing
    - ❏ Here: _____
- ❏ Fishing:
    - ❏ Fly
    - ❏ Spin
- ❏ Geocoaching
- ❏ Leather working
- ❏ Bowling:
    - ❏ Competitively
    - ❏ For fun
    - ❏ For the companionship and beer

(list continues . . .)

- *Routines* - *(continued)*

- ❑ Martial arts:
    - ❑ Karate
    - ❑ Judo
    - ❑ Something else: _____

_____

- ❑ Wine/beer/whiskey/scotch tasting
- ❑ Gourmet food
- ❑ Flying/parachuting/hang gliding
- ❑ Debating/politics
- ❑ Gambling
- ❑ Blogging/writing
- ❑ Paintball
- ❑ Brewing beer or wine
- ❑ Painting
- ❑ Running/biking/endurance work
- ❑ Renaissance fairs or period play acting
- ❑ This: _____

_____

_____

Us When We Communicate

– *Communication* –

I'd rather make our plans through:
- ❏ Phone calls
- ❏ Text messages
- ❏ I.M.
- ❏ E-mail
- ❏ In person:
    - ❏ On the spot
    - ❏ Ahead of time
    - ❏ Depends on the plan

When we communicate, please be:
- ❏ Frank
- ❏ Gentle
- ❏ Open to humor
- ❏ Affectionate
- ❏ A good listener
- ❏ Encouraging
- ❏ This: _____

Frankly, I'd rather that
- ❏ I make:
    - ❏ Most
    - ❏ All of the plans:
        - ❏ So I can surprise you
        - ❏ Because I'm a control freak
        - ❏ Because: _____

_____

- *Communication - (continued)*

❑ You make:
  ❑ Most
  ❑ All of the plans:
    ❑ Because you come up with really good ideas
    ❑ Because you're a control freak
    ❑ Because I don't really care what we do or where we go
    ❑ Because: _____
    _____
    _____

Love notes are:
  ❑ Fantastic and I really love getting them:
    ❑ When I get home
    ❑ In my bag
    ❑ Somewhere surprising
  ❑ Not really my favorites

If you write me love notes, please make them:
  ❑ Sentimental
  ❑ Admiring
  ❑ Erotic
  ❑ Something else: _____
  _____
  _____

- *Communication - (continued)*

While we're talking, I feel most comfortable when you:
- ❏ Listen without interrupting me
- ❏ Interject your thoughts and confirmation
- ❏ Keep eye contact
- ❏ Keep the conversation simple
- ❏ Reassure me with touches
- ❏ Bring up topics that are fun or interesting to both of us
- ❏ Something else: _____

_____

_____

 # *Us In Public*

– *In Public* –

When you look at me, I feel:
- ❏ Contented
- ❏ Aroused
- ❏ Joyful
- ❏ Enchanted
- ❏ In love
- ❏ Cute
- ❏ Handsome
- ❏ Taller
- ❏ Strong
- ❏ Other: _____

When we are out with our friends, I feel:
- ❏ Taller
- ❏ Happier
- ❏ More of a man
- ❏ Honored, especially when you:
  - ❏ Wear a dress
  - ❏ Wear perfume
  - ❏ Take my arm
  - ❏ Flirt with me
  - ❏ Say my name with your special voice
  - ❏ Show off how smart you are
  - ❏ Listen to my stories even though you've heard them

    (list continues . . .)

- In Public - (continued)

❏ Pose for me and others with that gorgeous body of yours
❏ Stand up for me
❏ Stand up for yourself
❏ Horse around
❏ Make everyone feel included
❏ Something else: _____

_____

When we're out with others, I wish you would:
❏ Let me make an ass of myself
❏ Stay near me
❏ Let me visit with others
❏ Flirt with others so they can see you going home with me
❏ Charm others like you charm me
❏ Show off your fantastic:
　❏ Body
　❏ Mind
　❏ Wallet
　❏ This: _____

_____

❏ Get just as playful as I'm getting
❏ Demonstrate your dignity
❏ Take care of me
❏ Something else: _____

_____

- In Public - (continued)

My favorite place for you to touch me in public is:
- ❑ My shoulder
- ❑ My back
- ❑ My arm
- ❑ My knee
- ❑ This spot: _____

_____

I:
- ❑ Love
- ❑ Am not much into:
    - ❑ You wearing expensive perfume, like: _____

    _____

    - ❑ You wearing a natural scent, like: _____

    _____

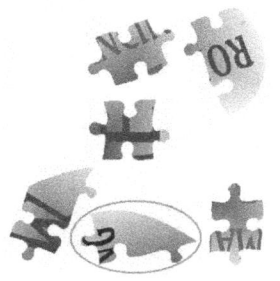

What You Do That I Adore

– *What I Adore* –

The outfit you wear that's my favorite is: _____

_____

You spoil me like mad when you:
- ❏ Listen
- ❏ Let me put my head on your lap
- ❏ Help me pick out flattering clothes
- ❏ Give me a backrub
- ❏ Make me a snack or meal
- ❏ Clean for me
- ❏ Tantalize me with your body

❏ Take care of my: _____

_____

❏ Something else: _____

_____

_____

The thing you do that is the biggest turn on for me is: _____

_____

_____

_____

- *What I Adore - (continued)*

I love it most when you:

- ❑ Suggest my favorite restaurant for our dates
- ❑ Offer to stay home instead of going out
- ❑ Buy me tickets to that performance I love
- ❑ Watch my favorite movie with me
- ❑ Bring over my favorite food/drink
- ❑ Brag about me on your social network page
- ❑ Challenge my mind
- ❑ Beat me at _____
- ❑ Share your day or your feelings
- ❑ Rip my clothes off
- ❑ This: _____

_____

_____

_____

Us At Home

– *At Home* –

The way I'd want you to wake me is:
- ❏ Please don't, you know how grumpy I am
- ❏ Bring coffee
- ❏ Kiss me
- ❏ Bring food: _____

When we are having a quiet evening or day at home, I'd really rather:
- ❏ Sit around like a slug
- ❏ Cuddle
- ❏ Watch my favorite TV: _____
  _____
- ❏ Play a:
  - ❏ Video game
    - ❏ With you
    - ❏ By myself
  - ❏ Board game
  - ❏ Card game
- ❏ Stay in bed:
  - ❏ Until we're both in the mood to make love
  - ❏ Until we're both too hungry to stay
  - ❏ Until it's time for my favorite TV
  - ❏ Until: _____
  _____

(list continues . . .)

- At Home - (continued)

❏ Sit and read:
   ❏ To you
   ❏ With you
   ❏ Next to you
❏ Snuggle with our laptops, iPads, or iPhones and keep each other company

I also:

❏ Like pets
❏ Have a pet
❏ Am not into pets
❏ Something else: _____

_____

I am a:

❏ Long, hot bath man
❏ Short shower man
❏ Singing in the shower man
❏ Shower with my girl man

Us When We Eat

– *When We Eat* –

Around food and romance, I prefer:
- ❑ Eating out:
    - ❑ The cuisine doesn't matter:
        - ❑ As long as the food is good
        - ❑ As long as the restaurant is fancy
        - ❑ As long as I'm seen with you
        - ❑ As long as you like it
        - ❑ As long as the meals are
            - ❑ Generous
            - ❑ Healthy
    - ❑ For restaurants, I really like:
        - ❑ Sports bars/pub food
        - ❑ Steak houses/chop shops
        - ❑ Hamburgers
        - ❑ Pizza
        - ❑ Wings
        - ❑ Sandwich shops
        - ❑ Diners
        - ❑ Ethnic or international: _ _____
        - ❑ Family restaurants
        - ❑ Healthy
        - ❑ Vegetarian
        - ❑ Vegan

(list continues . . .)

- When We Eat - (continued)

- ❏ Something nearby
- ❏ Someplace hard to get a reservation for
- ❏ Someplace quiet and intimate
- ❏ Elegant
- ❏ Bistros
- ❏ Upscale
- ❏ My own style: _____

❏ Eating at home, and:
- ❏ I cook
- ❏ You cook

❏ Eating at home and ordering in:
- ❏ Pizza
- ❏ Sandwiches
- ❏ Chinese
- ❏ Italian
- ❏ Indian
- ❏ Mexican
- ❏ Something else: _____

My favorite meal that you:
- ❏ Make
- ❏ Buy
- ❏ Eat that I make

is: _____

_____

- When We Eat - (continued)

This is my favorite dessert: _____

I am:

    ❏ A wine drinker with meals
    ❏ A beer drinker with meals
    ❏ A Scotch drinker with meals, and this is my brand of Scotch:

    _____

    ❏ A mixed drink man:

    _____

    ❏ Something else:

    _____

When I'm eating, I really prefer:

    ❏ Formal dining – even at home I like linen on the table.
    ❏ Casual dining
    ❏ Totally casual dining –just hand me my plate and then move so I can watch TV
    ❏ Adventurous dining, including picnics or mystery theatre
    ❏ Barbecuing with friends or family

 *Us Apart*

– *Apart* –

- I like to carry a memento of us with me when I'm away from you:
    - A lock of your hair
    - The last note you wrote me
    - A photo of us
    - A photo of you
    - Something else:_____
- Instead, I think of memories of our time together as the best mementos

When we're apart for a period of time, I like to:
- Have a phone call with you at a set time
- Send you surprise texts or e-mails from time to time
- Think fondly of you while I concentrate on what I'm away for

When I'm not with my girl, I'm the kind of man who:
- Focuses on the job at hand
- Buys little presents for my girl
- Likes to know where you are and what you're up to
- Works hard at getting back to you
- Hangs out with the guys to have a balanced life

 # *Us and Gifts*

– *Gifts* –

I prefer goods:
- ❏ Jewelry
- ❏ Scents
- ❏ Food
- ❏ Games/electronics
- ❏ Things for my house:_____
  _____

- ❏ Clothing
- ❏ Books
- ❏ You in a red ribbon
- ❏ Something for my hobby:
- ❏ Tickets to: _____
  _____

- ❏ Gift cards for:_____
  _____

- ❏ A pet:_____
- ❏ A trip to:_____
  _____

- ❏ Sporting goods like:_____
  _____

About flowers – I:
- ❏ Like flowers
- ❏ Am not much into flowers

(list continues . . .)

- Gifts - (continued)

- ❏ My favorite flowers are: _____
  _____
- ❏ You can send me flowers at work
- ❏ Please send me flowers only at home
- ❏ You can send me flowers even though I live with my parents
- ❏ Please don't send me flowers
  - ❏ But you can bring some
  - ❏ And don't bring any, either

I prefer services:
- ❏ Would love a massage:
  - ❏ That you give me
  - ❏ That you buy for me
- ❏ Buy me a:
  - ❏ Personal trainer
  - ❏ Coach to have a better _____ _____ game
- ❏ Day at the:
  - ❏ Spa
  - ❏ Circus
  - ❏ Beach
  - ❏ Shopping
  - ❏ Ski slope
  - ❏ Beach
  - ❏ Zoo
  - *(list continues . . .)*

- Gifts - (continued)

  - ❏ Races
  - ❏ Horse
  - ❏ Dog
  - ❏ Car
  - ❏ Bicycle
  - ❏ People
  - ❏ Extreme
  - ❏ Triathlon
  - ❏ Boats
  - ❏ Something else: _____

  _____

- ❏ Game/match _____
- ❏ Fair/festival: _____
- ❏ Museum: _____
- ❏ Farm/ranch:_____
- ❏ Park:
  - ❏ Amusement
  - ❏ State
  - ❏ Bike/skateboard
  - ❏ Snowboard
- ❏ Range:
  - ❏ Shooting
  - ❏ Archery
  - ❏ Something else: _____

_____

(list continues . . .)

- Gifts - (continued)

- ❏ Clean my:
    - ❏ House
    - ❏ Garage
        - ❏ Car
    - ❏ Office
    - ❏ Something else: _____
- ❏ Give me a free night out with my friends:
    - ❏ Every once in awhile
    - ❏ Often

I prefer clothing:
- ❏ Please don't buy me clothes; I'm better at buying my own
- ❏ I love receiving these kinds of clothing from my girl:
    - ❏ Hats
    - ❏ Jackets:
        - ❏ Outdoor:
            - ❏ Formal
            - ❏ Casual
        - ❏ Office
        - ❏ Casual
    - ❏ Suits
    - ❏ Shirts:
        - ❏ Work
        - ❏ Play
    - ❏ Ties

(list continues . . .)

- Gifts - (continued)

- ❏ Cuff links
- ❏ Pants/Slacks:
  - ❏ Work
  - ❏ Play
- ❏ Belts
- ❏ Underwear:
  - ❏ T-shirts
  - ❏ Boxers
  - ❏ Briefs
  - ❏ Feel free to buy me something spicy
- ❏ Socks
- ❏ Shoes

When I buy you gifts, please:
- ❏ Let me know honestly whether you like them
- ❏ Know that I thought a lot about them before giving them to you
- ❏ Appreciate my gifts no matter what

The gift I wish I could get for you, but:
- ❏ Can't afford to
- ❏ Am not sure you would like
- ❏ Would need more information from you before getting

   is this: _____

   _____

 # Us and Sex

– *Sex* –

- ❑ Sexually, I am:
    - ❑ Romantic
    - ❑ Hot and fast
    - ❑ Playful
    - ❑ Teasing
    - ❑ Rough

- ❑ About BDSM, I:
    - ❑ Don't know what that is
    - ❑ Have experimented
    - ❑ Like the idea
    - ❑ Have a dungeon in my house
        - ❑ I am:
            - ❑ A Top
            - ❑ A Bottom
            - ❑ A Versatile
            - ❑ I don't know what that is

I like to have sex:
- ❑ At home where it's private
- ❑ In places where we might get caught
- ❑ Out in nature
- ❑ All over the house
- ❑ In water
- ❑ In my vehicle
- ❑ In your vehicle

(list continues . . .)

- Sex - (continued)

❏ On the phone
❏ On-line
❏ Here: _____

Here is my one favorite position:_____

_____

Here is the one thing I've wanted to try with you and haven't mentioned it yet: _____

_____

_____

The longest time I've had sex continuously was:
    ❏ Counted in hours
    ❏ Counted in days
    ❏ It's not the time, it's the quality that counts

During sex, I like to add:
    ❏ Food that we can play with
    ❏ Gels or lotions
    ❏ Tantalizing clothing: _____
    _____
    ❏ Role playing
    ❏ Soft fabrics
    ❏ Rough fabrics and items
    (list continues . . .)

- Sex - (continued)

- ❏ Dirty language
- ❏ Erotic but sweet language
- ❏ Music
- ❏ Ice
- ❏ Candle wax
- ❏ Blindfolds
- ❏ Handcuffs or other binding equipment
- ❏ Another person: _____

_____

- ❏ Video/Photographs
- ❏ Pornography
- ❏ Something else: _____

_____

What sex means to me is that it:
- ❏ Shares love with you
- ❏ Shows you and me how beautiful we are
- ❏ Offers a playful way to be intimate
- ❏ Shares our love of God or our Creator
- ❏ Celebrates our relationship
- ❏ Relieves stress
- ❏ Makes me feel handsome or good looking

The most sexually attractive part of you is your: _

_____

- Sex - (continued)

Here is one more thing I want to tell you about our lovemaking:

_____

_____

_____

_____

Wrap-up: Tell Her How You Feel

This page is for you to share anything at all with your girl. If you're stuck for words, just name the song that would do it for you. Well done!

About the Author

Marianne Pelletier is a certified tarot reader and practicing psychic, as well as a fund-raiser for a large university. Marianne's writing on romance and flirting, management, wealth building, and personal journeys appear in various formats, from small poetry magazines to Helium.com and triond.com.

She lives in Upstate New York with her partner, Laura.

www.ingramcontent.com/pod-product-compliance
Lightning Source LLC
Chambersburg PA
CBHW071750040426
42446CB00012B/2509